Rachel Mackinnon

BIRDS

A WARD LOCK BOOK

First published in the UK 1996
by Ward Lock
Wellington House
125 Strand
LONDON
WC2R 0BB

A Cassell Imprint

Original title of the book in Spanish:
El Fascinante Mundo de Las Aves

© Copyright Parramón Ediciones,
S.A. - World Rights
Published by Parramón Ediciones,
S.A., Barcelona, Spain

Author: Maria Ángels Julivert
Illustrator: Francisco Arrendondo

English translation © Copyright 1992
Barron's Educational Series, Inc.

Distributed in Australia
by Capricorn Link (Australia) Pty Ltd
2/13 Carrington Road, Castle Hill NSW 2154

A British Library Cataloguing in Publication Data block for
this book may be obtained from the British Library.

ISBN Hardback 0 7063 7547 5
      Paperback 0 7063 7553 X
Printed and bound in Spain

THE FASCINATING WORLD OF...

BIRDS

by

Maria Ángels Julivert

Illustrations by Francisco Arredondo

WARD LOCK

BIRDS: CONQUERORS OF THE AIR

After fish, birds are the largest and most varied group of **vertebrates**—animals that have backbones. There are 9,000 species, which have adapted to conditions in almost every part of the world.

A bird's body is covered with feathers, some of which may be beautifully coloured. Only the beak and, generally, also the feet are bare. Outer feathers, called contour feathers or **penneae**, as well as the underlying down feathers, or **plumulae**, keep the birds warm and protect them from the sun's rays.

The wings and tail of a bird have long, flexible flight feathers. Those of the upper and lower wing surfaces are called **primaries** and **secondaries**. The tail flight feathers are known as **rectrices**. As their name suggests, flight feathers are essential for flight. Smaller feathers, which cover the bases of the flight feathers, are called **coverts.**

Most birds fly by beating their wings. Others, such as the eagle, take advantage of air currents to glide or soar in the skies. The most astonishing flight method, however, is that of the hummingbird. It is able to hover in the air, and it can fly backwards as well as make abrupt changes of direction.

Some birds, like the ostrich, have lost their ability to fly. Others, like the penguin, use their modified wings as flippers to propel themselves in the water.

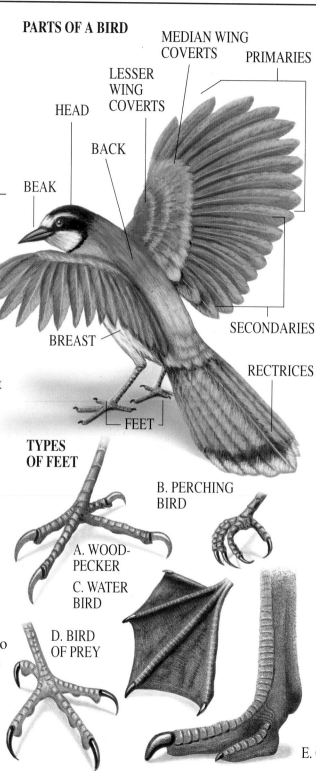

PARTS OF A BIRD

MEDIAN WING COVERTS

PRIMARIES

LESSER WING COVERTS

HEAD

BACK

BEAK

SECONDARIES

BREAST

RECTRICES

FEET

TYPES OF FEET

A. WOODPECKER

B. PERCHING BIRD

C. WATER BIRD

D. BIRD OF PREY

E. OSTRICH

Right: The hummingbird is the smallest bird in the world. It is also unique because of its distinctive flight: the extremely rapid beating of its wings lets it hover in the air as it sips nectar from a flower with its long beak.

Left: A bird's feet are adapted to its way of life. The feet of climbing birds (A) help them climb tree trunks. Those of perching birds (B) let them hold onto the branches. Water birds (C) have webbing between their toes that helps them swim. Birds of prey (D) have toes that are curved to hold small animals. The ostrich (E) has only two toes, which help it run very fast.

GREAT BUILDERS

To protect their eggs and young, most birds build a **nest** using their beaks as their only tool. The shape and size of these nests differ greatly. Some species build truly remarkable structures. Nesting sites include the ground, trees, and even inside cacti.

There are also birds that don't build nests at all. They lay their eggs in vegetation, on the rocky ledges of steep cliffs, or on the bare ground.

The golden oriole lives in the forests and builds a fascinating nest by skilfully weaving together thin strips of grass, plant stems, and other materials. These spectacular structures hang from the tree branches in the shape of a basket.

Golden orioles spend the winter in Africa, but in April they travel a long distance to their breeding grounds in Europe and Asia. The first to arrive are the males, who have splendid **plumage**. Each bird establishes its own territory. These are also the first to migrate back to warmer climates. Northern (or Baltimore) orioles winter in Mexico and Central America.

NORTHERN OR BALTIMORE ORIOLE

Right: Some birds place their nests in the most unlikely spots. This type of woodpecker nests inside giant cacti. It uses its beak to make the cavity, as the right side of the illustration shows.

Left: The northern and golden orioles build suspended woven nests.

GOLDEN ORIOLE

ANYTHING GOES

Birds use a wide variety of materials in their building. Small branches and dry grass are usually the main elements of many nests. Some birds even use bits of paper, string, or plastic.

They line the inside of the nests with feathers, hair, and wool to make it warm and comfortable.

The long-tailed tit uses mosses, lichens, and cobwebs. The penduline tit builds with cobwebs.

The job of gathering the right materials and building the nest is hard work. Usually both the male and the female share this job. However, in a few species, only one of the pair does all of the work.

Generally, each pair builds its own nest. Sociable weavers, however, construct spectacular apartment houses. These small birds form large groups and together build a very large structure with many entrance holes, all of which face down towards the ground.

The nest increases in size as new pairs join the group. It can measure more than 9 feet (3 m) in length and may accommodate more than a hundred birds. The tops of acacia trees are the preferred location for these lodgings.

Right: The penduline tit builds its nest with only one opening (see top right of illustration). The nest in the foreground shows a cross-section of the interior with the female sitting on her eggs.

Left: Nest of the long-tailed tit built with moss and cobwebs.

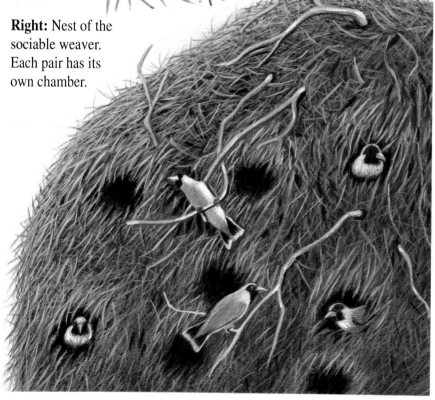

Right: Nest of the sociable weaver. Each pair has its own chamber.

COURTSHIP BEHAVIOUR

Reproduction, which ensures the continuation of the species, is one of the most important stages in a bird's life. During this period, the plumage of the males, which they proudly display to the females, becomes more colourful than usual.

The peacock fans out its long, beautifully iridescent tail feathers to attract the hen. The male frigate bird inflates its throat pouch for the same reason.

During **courtship**, many birds perform fascinating dances. In some species, for example the grebes, both male and female take part in the dance, whereas in others, only the male does the "dancing."

Grebes perform their acrobatics in the water. The partners face one another, stretch their necks, and move their heads from side to side; they also tempt each other with offerings of tasty water plants.

Once a pair bond is formed, nest building begins. Grebes form a large floating platform, which is often anchored to the plants around it. There the female lays her eggs. After a number of days the chicks **hatch**. The young are ferried about and fed on the backs of their parents.

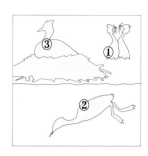

Right: A pair of European crested grebes ① performing their courtship dance, during which they offer each other food—water plants they pluck out of the river or lake bottom ②. Afterward, the female incubates her eggs by sitting on the floating nest ③. The Western grebe of North America performs a similar dance.

MALE FRIGATE BIRD

FEMALE FRIGATE BIRD

FEMALE RUFF (REEVE)

MALE RUFF

Above and left: Two examples of courting behaviour. The male frigate bird of southern Florida and Louisiana (above) inflates its red throat pouch; the male ruff (left) displays a magnificent collar of feathers.

COURTING STRUCTURES

A few birds do more than just build a nest. In certain species as the breeding season approaches, each male claims a small territory. There, he builds a complex structure to attract potential mates.

Bowerbirds weave branches and grass strips around tree trunks to form towers that may be more than 6 feet (2 m) high. Others prepare a clearing on the ground, which they carefully tend and also decorate with leaves laid upside down.

Some bowerbirds even make pathways with branches and grasses. The male covers a short walkway with these materials and also builds a low wall on either side. These birds also decorate the walls with different colourful objects, such as flowers, fruit, shells, and even pieces of glass or plastic. Some bowerbirds varnish the walls with a substance made of saliva mixed with crushed fruit.

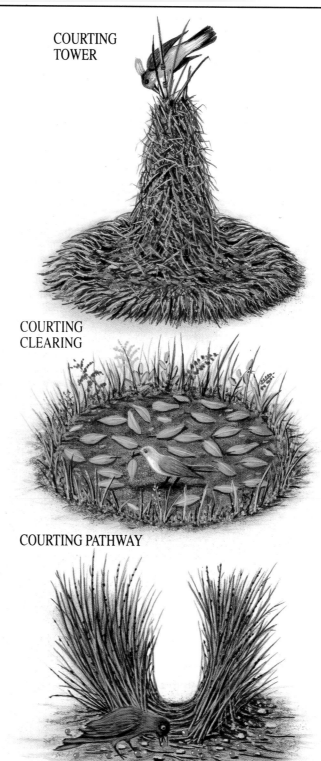

COURTING TOWER

COURTING CLEARING

COURTING PATHWAY

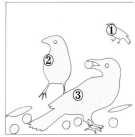

Right: Courting structures are reserved exclusively for courting potential mates. The males of the Australian bowerbird create pathways through which they walk for displaying ①; they decorate the walls with saliva and crushed fruit ②. To attract a female, they cover the ground with berries or other fruits, and feathers ③.

Left: Courting structures vary according to species: they may be towers more than 6 feet (2 m) high, ground clearings decorated with leaves, or pathways formed with woven twigs and branches.

CARING FOR THE YOUNG

All birds lay eggs, whose shape, size, and colour vary greatly among species. Likewise, the number of eggs in a **clutch** can differ: Some birds lay a single egg, others lay many.

The young of many species are born totally defenceless, often without down and with their eyes closed. Such chicks are called **nidicolous**. They are totally dependent on their parents for a long time. Others, by contrast, called **nidifugous**, have a covering of soft down that keeps them warm. They are well-developed and leave the nest from a few hours to two days after hatching.

Usually both parents feed and look after the chicks. In some species only the female does so. Chicks are greedy eaters. They chirp incessantly and beg for food with gaping beaks.

A few species manage to slip their eggs into the nests of other birds, generally one smaller than itself. For example, the European cuckoo lays several eggs in the nests of other species, but deposits only one per nest. The host birds nearly always **incubate** the foreign egg. Upon hatching, the cuckoo chick throws all eggs and other hatchlings out of the nest. The North American yellow- and black-billed cuckoos, however, rarely lay their eggs in the nests of other species. Occasionally, they do lay eggs in the nests of other cuckoos.

BURROWING OWL   JACKDAW

OSPREY   OSTRICH

DIFFERENT TYPES OF EGGS

ADULT OF A DIFFERENT SPECIES

CUCKOO CHICK

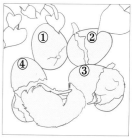

Right: Birds reproduce by laying eggs, which are incubated between 10 to 65 days, according to the species. The chick breaks open the egg with its egg tooth, a little device at the end of its upper bill ①. Then it enlarges the opening ② – ③, and finally hatches ④.

Left: The European cuckoo deposits its eggs in the nests of other birds. The host birds are tricked into incubating the foreign egg. The cuckoo chick, although considerably larger than its foster parents, will also be fed by them.

FEEDING TIME

Birds eat a great variety of animals and plants. They swallow their food whole because they have no teeth for chewing.

The size and shape of a bird's beak can vary according to its diet. Seed eaters need a strong, short bill to crack seeds and grains; they may also swallow small pebbles for grinding the seed.

Some birds eat fruits, and others, such as the long-billed hummingbird, sip nectar from flowers.

Insects are preferred by many species, and a few, like the crows and magpies, are **omnivores**—they will eat anything.

Carnivores will catch reptiles as well as small mammals. Some, like owls, bring up or **regurgitate** the indigestible parts, such as bone, hair, and feathers, all pressed together into a small **pellet**.

Some birds have very specialized diets. For example, the osprey feeds almost exclusively on fish.

During the breeding season, adult birds must provide food for their offspring, especially those whose chicks are nidicolous.

In contrast, shortly after birth nidifugous chicks are able to follow their parents in search of food.

SEVERAL BEAK SHAPES

SEED EATER: HAWFINCH

INSECTIVORE: EUROPEAN BEE EATER

OMNIVORE: BLACK-BILLED MAGPIE

CARNIVORE: PEREGRINE FALCON

Right: Nidicolous chicks ① are unable to survive on their own and remain in the nest a long time ②. There they are fed by their parents, as this jay is shown doing ③. The jay is a European bird that is closely related to the North American bluejay.

Above: The shape and size of the beaks of different species are the result of adaptation to the type of food each eats.

Right: The osprey dives into the water to catch fish; it then surfaces to continue its powerful flight.

AVIAN FORTRESSES

Birds use different strategies to protect their offspring from predators. Some species conceal their nests and eggs through camouflage.

The European nuthatch nests in tree cavities, often taking advantage of abandoned woodpecker holes. This small bird takes the unique precaution of closing off the entrance to its nest with mud, leaving only a small entrance hole.

A more secure and impregnable shelter is that of many hornbills. The females of these species enclose themselves inside a tree hole with their eggs. Only a narrow crack large enough for their bills is left open. Through this crack the male will pass food to the female. The females mix saliva with mud, food remnants, and faeces to make a paste. When it dries, this mixture becomes hard and is long lasting. In some hornbill species the male assists in sealing the nest.

Many ground-nesting birds pretend to be injured as a means of protecting their young. The adult attracts the attention of the predator to lead it away from the nest. It cries out loudly and pretends it has a broken wing by dragging it. This performance never fails to convince a predator, which greedily follows the bird believing it an easy prey.

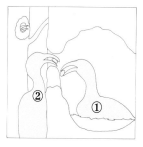

Right: The female ① of the hornbill walls herself into the nest cavity to incubate her eggs. She leaves an opening through which the male ② can feed her and provide her with the materials for sealing the wall.

Left: A strategy used by some birds to safeguard their nests is to draw a predator's attention to themselves by pretending to have a broken wing.

Right: The cross section shows a European nuthatch nest inside a tree cavity; the female is feeding her young.

SKILFUL WEAVERS

Several species have developed great skill in weaving nests out of plant materials. Some of them excel at this.

The weavers are skilful birds who hang their complex nests from tree branches. These remarkable structures are made with grass and other strips of plant material which the bird weaves with its bill and feet.

This is an activity done only by the male. Little by little he interlaces the fibres to form the nest chamber. At one end he makes a long tube for entering the nest.

The great reed warbler nests among the tall reeds in ponds not far from the water. It builds a basket by wrapping different kinds of vegetation around a few reed stems.

Another warbler, the tailorbird, constructs a nest that is unparalleled in the avian world. It sews anywhere from two to a number of leaves together. First, using its bill, it punctures the borders of the leaves. Then it passes thin strands of grass through the holes and knots them to prevent them from loosening. The leaves are joined halfway up. It then fills the hole with plant materials.

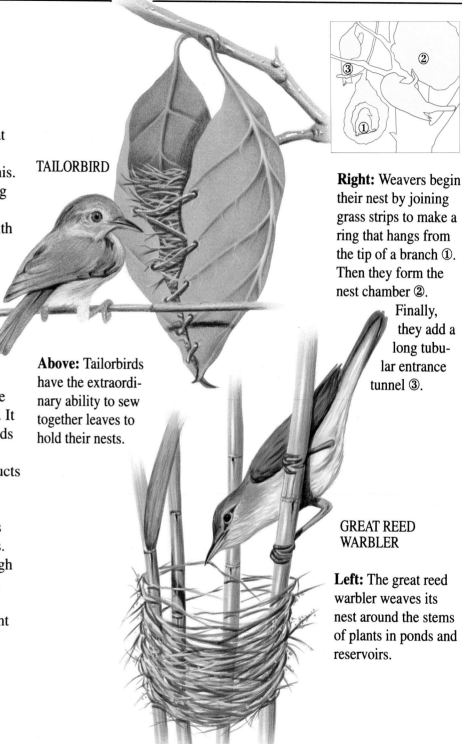

TAILORBIRD

Above: Tailorbirds have the extraordinary ability to sew together leaves to hold their nests.

Right: Weavers begin their nest by joining grass strips to make a ring that hangs from the tip of a branch ①. Then they form the nest chamber ②. Finally, they add a long tubular entrance tunnel ③.

GREAT REED WARBLER

Left: The great reed warbler weaves its nest around the stems of plants in ponds and reservoirs.

AVIAN MINERS

Only a few species dig burrows in the ground for nesting. Among the more outstanding **avian** diggers are the bee eaters and the kingfishers. These birds build their nests in dry sand banks.

With their sharp bills, the male and female carve out an entrance tunnel that opens up into a small oval nest chamber. The pair work together in the construction of their shelter. Using their feet, they push out the loose soil from the hole.

The nestlings, which are born blind and without feathers, are well protected within the chamber.

Bee eaters catch flying insects in midair. When they take a bee or hornet they remove the sting before swallowing it. Groups of bee eaters nest together, sometimes forming very large **colonies**.

Kingfishers are solitary nesters. They carve out their nests in a section of a river far from others of their kind.

The exclusive food of the kingfisher is fish, which it catches by diving into the water. Once out of the water, it whacks its prey against a hard surface before gulping it down.

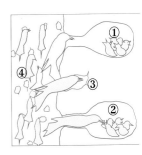

A. KINGFISHER HITTING A FISH AGAINST A ROCK

Left and below: True to its name, the feisty kingfisher fishes in rivers. Once it has caught a fish, it then smashes it against a branch or rock (A), before feeding it to its chicks (B).

Right: Cross section of nests of the European bee eater. Parent birds take turns feeding the nestlings ① – ② and digging new chambers ③.
Left: Front view of a rock wall full of nests of the carmine bee eater ④.

B. SECTION OF A KINGFISHER'S NEST

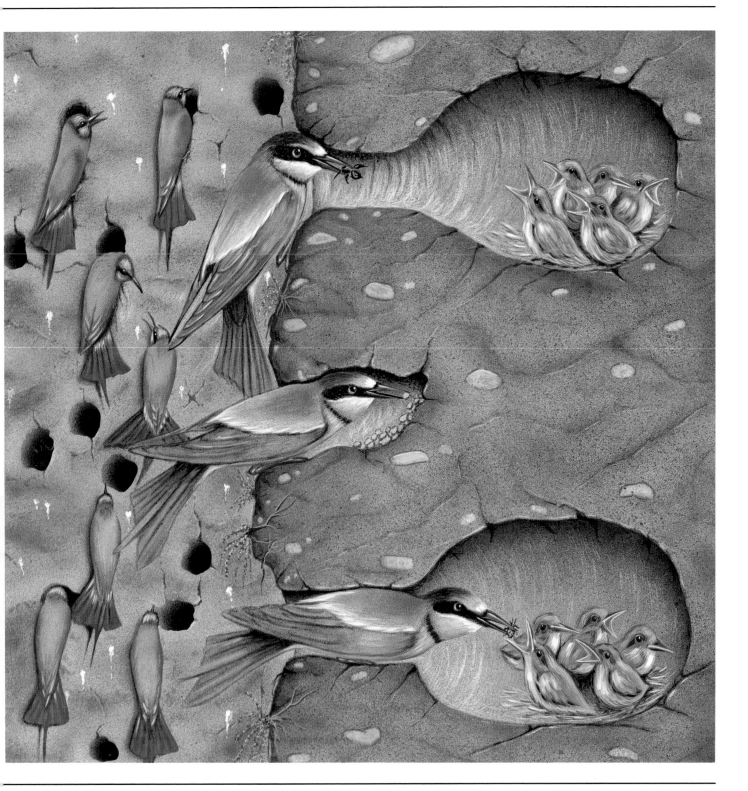

MASTER CARPENTERS

BEAK AND FOOT OF A WOODPECKER

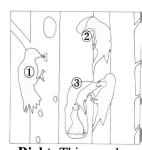

Woodpeckers are true artists when it comes to working with wood. Using their sturdy, pointed beaks, they drill the tree trunks to carve out their nests.

Both male and female share in this difficult task that keeps them busy for several days. The bottom of the cavity contains a layer of fine wood shavings on which the female lays her eggs.

Right: This woodpecker ① stores food in the holes it previously drilled in the trunk of a tree. In the nests they carve out of a tree ②, woodpeckers feed and care for their chicks ③.

Top left: The sharp and strong bill of the woodpecker is an excellent tool for chiselling wood. Its feet, with its opposing pairs of toes, allow the bird to climb tree trunks easily.

A woodpecker's foot has four toes that are equipped with very sharp claws. Two toes face forward and two backward. This gives the bird strength for clinging and climbing with incredible ease. Its tail feathers are very stiff and strong. When pressed against a tree surface, the tail actually helps support the bird.

The woodpecker's repeated pecking on the tree trunks produces a drumming sound that can be heard a considerable distance away.

Woodpeckers drill the bark of tree trunks in search of insects and larvae that live there. They also eat seeds and fruits.

To survive the winter, some woodpeckers prepare a storeroom to keep food. In a dead tree, they drill several holes which they then fill with acorns, nuts, or other foods. Each hollow will hold a single item.

Above: The interior of a tree trunk is a warm and comfortable refuge for the young of the woodpecker.

AVIAN MASONS

A few bird species place their nests in structures built by humans. Some owls like to lay their eggs in old abandoned barns, attics, and so on. Storks like to build their enormous nests on top of chimneys or bell towers. A few swallows and martins hang their nests on beams, walls, or under the eaves or cornices of buildings.

Swallows gather mud from puddles and shape it with their bills into small balls, which they use for building their bowl-shaped nests. They also use straw and feathers in their construction.

Martins make a more elaborate structure. Their nest is a small, closed receptacle with only a narrow opening at the top.

Of the few birds that use mud, the rufus ovenbird is decidedly the master.

The ovenbird builds a spherical nest with a mixture of clay, hair, and plant matter. Using its feet and beak, it carefully kneads this compound. After the mixture dries, it solidifies into a strong and hard material. The structure has very thick walls. Inside, the bird erects a dividing wall between the nest chamber and the entrance.

A. NEST OF THE MARTIN

B. NEST OF THE RUFUS OVENBIRD

C. NEST OF THE STORK

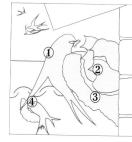

Right: This swallow ① feeds its hungry chicks ② that wait in the nest ③ attached to the wall of a building. Swallows use their bills to make mud balls for constructing their nests ④.

Left: The martin builds its round nest with mud and makes only one small entrance opening (A). The rufus ovenbird adds small twigs to the mud for strength (B). By contrast, the stork uses mud and feathers to erect its large saucer-shaped structure (C).

SEABIRDS

Birds have colonised many different environments: forests, plains, mountains, lakes, and rivers.

Many species live on or near the sea, from which they obtain their food.

Some birds always stay close to the shore. Others, like the albatross, spend most of their life over the open sea and travel great distances, ranging over thousands of miles.

Nevertheless, like all birds, they must approach land for nesting and rearing their young.

Ocean birds use islands, beaches, or rocky cliff ledges as nesting sites. A few species, such as the pelican, can even be found in inland waters.

Most seabirds form large colonies, which may consist of thousands of breeding pairs. The nests are generally close to one another, thus limiting the size of a pair's territory.

They build their nests with materials they can find close by. Many make a small mound of sand and grass for the female to lay her eggs on.

Above: A large platform constructed with dead branches on top of a tree supports the nest of the pelican.

Below: Pelicans feed in groups. The pouch under the bill is expandable and very useful for catching fish.

Right: The albatross travels thousands of miles to nest on coastal lands. It breeds in large colonies where the males engage in combat displays during courtship ① and the females lay their eggs ②. Each female incubates her own eggs and nurtures her young ③ in a nest built with soil and plant materials ④.

Glossary

avian. Referring to birds.

carnivore. Animal that feeds almost exclusively on other animals.

clutch. A small group of eggs or chicks.

colonies. Large groups formed by birds that nest together.

courtship. Behaviour of birds during the breeding season. Courting helps males and females find partners of the same species.

coverts. Shorter feathers that cover the bare quills of the longer flight feathers.

egg tooth. Sharp, hard point on the bill of a hatching bird. It is used to break a hole in the shell of the egg.

hatch. Birth of a young bird from an egg. The number, size, and colour of the eggs varies among different bird species.

incubate. To warm eggs by sitting on them. This stimulates the development of the embryo inside.

insectivore. Animal that feeds on insects.

nest. Structure for hatching and raising young.

nidicolous. Referring to chicks that live in the nest for a long time before becoming independent. Many of them are born without feathers and with their eyes closed.

nidifugous. Referring to chicks that leave the nest a few hours after hatching.

omnivore. Animal that feeds on other animals as well as plants.

pellets. Balls some birds regurgitate that consist of hair, feathers, bones, and other indigestible bits of food.

penneae. Outer feathers of a bird consisting of contour feathers and flight feathers.

plumage. Feathers that cover the body of a bird.

plumulae. Down feathers of a bird.

primaries. Flight feathers in the outer tip of the wing of a bird.

regurgitate. To bring up from the stomach food that cannot be digested.

rectrices. Flight feathers in the tail of a bird.

secondaries. Median flight feathers in the lower edge of the wing of a bird.

talon. A claw, especially of a bird of prey.

vertebrate. An animal that has a spinal column or backbone. Fish, amphibians, reptiles, birds, and mammals are vertebrates.

Index